THE CHANGING FACE OF SEAFORD

Patricia Berry and Steve Benz

S. B. Publications

First published in 2005 by S. B. Publications
Tel: 01323 893498
Email: sbpublications@tiscali.co.uk

ISBN 1-85770-299-9

Designed and Typeset by EH Graphics (01273) 515527
Printed by Ethos Productions Ltd.

Front cover photo: Terminus Road / Clinton Place.
Back cover photo: Aerial view of Seaford.

INTRODUCTION

The earliest picture among the following pages dates from the end of the nineteenth century, the latest photograph was taken only days before this book went to press. In the time in between, the population of Seaford has risen more than sevenfold, with relative increases in the volume of the housing, shops and public utilities needed to support such growth.

It says much for the foresight and wisdom of our ancestors that so much of the town standing a century ago has - barring accidents and enemy attack - still survived today. These are the examples where 'Then' and 'Now' are almost interchangeable; in others, buildings have altered so much that we cannot believe we are looking at the same structures.

It is these similarities and contrasts that, together with the evolving nature of the town and its inhabitants, have made the compiling of this book such an engrossing and enjoyable task.

Over the course of a thousand years Seaford has evolved from a tiny fishing village through local triumphs and disasters to become the community we know today. It has survived centuries of fierce storms and floods that rendered people homeless and repeatedly destroyed the shoreline, its inhabitants have been struck down with epidemics like the Black Death in the 14th century and the worldwide influenza after the First World War. Alarms have sounded more than once as invasion loomed, and cross-Channel raiders have several times left the little town in smoking ruins. Enough to make any population lose heart and turn to wrecking, smuggling and piracy!

Victorian incomers saw the area as ripe for development into a 'second Brighton' for visitors, but the best-laid plans (like the causeway roads to link the sea-front with the town) came to next to nothing. Their envisaged enlargements and improvements almost all took place within the span of this book.

ACKNOWLEDGEMENTS

Over the last twenty years, there have been at least eight illustrated books published on Seaford using postcards and photographs. New illustrative material is being discovered all the time due to the diligence of local historians and postcard collectors. One of the main reasons for producing this book was to publish these latest finds, many of which have never been published before.

The authors would like to thank John Eastlake for giving kind permission to use a number of his photographs, some of which are very rare. Also thanks to Lindsay Woods for taking several of the 'Now' photographs at very short notice.

We would like to thank everyone who has in any way helped with the compilation of this book and apologise if any source has not been cleared. We hope that no one will be distressed by finding themselves or past family and friends included, and will be pleased to have comments from interested parties.

THE CHANGING FACE OF SEAFORD

SEAFORD HEAD Crowned by the remains of an Iron Age fortress, the cliffs have meant disaster to off course ships, stranded walkers and over eager egg-hunting school boys. Eroded by nature and by man (see changing profile in following pages), they present an on-going challenge to sea defence schemes like the concrete tripods illustrated below.

SHIPWRECKS Dangerous cross-currents and bad weather in notorious Seaford Bay have caused many disasters. The SS 'Newstead', Capetown to Hamburg, ran aground in dense fog. The Newhaven relief lifeboat rescued all aboard. Similarly be-fogged in early summer 1936, the 2500-ton Russian 'Ussuri' was stranded opposite the Salts recreation ground, lying there till a sister ship arrived to tow her off. The ship's pet monkey and cats are remembered by some older Seaforders.

SHIPWRECKS cont'd. 23rd December 1988 saw the Belgian trawler 'White Horse' aground opposite the Buckle Inn. Efforts to refloat her were made by the fire brigade and Newhaven tugs, witnessed over Christmas by many visitors. A gale on 21st October 1998 stranded the Dutch sailing ship 'Eendracht' near Tide Mills. Dramatic helicopter rescues of its fifty-one trainee sailors were seen on national television.

SEAFORD HEAD.

SPLASH POINT Developed from a convalescent home for a doctor's son, Splash Point Hotel was demolished after compulsory purchase in the 1960s. Following erosion of the cliff face, hotel ground within the brick wall was needed for a new public footpath. The long groyne was built was built at an estimated cost of £650,000.

SPLASH POINT. SEAFORD.

MARTELLO TOWER Built around 1810 as a defence against a Napoleonic assault that never came, the dry-moated tower thereafter stood neglected till bought by Mr Tom Funell for transformation into an amusement centre. Since 1979 the tower, restored as nearly as practicable to its original has housed Seaford Museum.

ESPLANADE The 1950s view near the Esplanade Hotel of a typical busy beach and promenade includes three pupils from Annecy Convent in their distinctive sportswear, deckchairs complete with canvas canopies and more of Mr Simmons' chairs stored in old 'sentry box' changing tents. Permanent concrete-walled beach huts were installed by the local authority in place of pre-war wooden ones.

Martello Tower towards Splash Point, Seaford 26049

ESPLANADE cont'd. In the background, the Martello tower sports on its seaward side the gleaming white shelter where visitors could sit, out of reach of the famous Seaford sea breezes. From time to time refreshments were available from a café there. Shortly before demolition, it screened an amusement arcade with fruit machines. Groynes and steps to the beach also gave shelter.

SEAFRONT from the gun platform of the Martello Tower, the upper view shows the post-recharging scheme beach (1987), no longer with the individuality of its former groyne-divided, roughly piled shingle days. The nine million pound scheme saved the seafront from destruction in the great hurricane and allowed development of housing closer to the sea, where none had been safe before.

ESPLANADE HOTEL/MALLETT CLOSE The easterly part of the hotel opened in 1891, the French chateau tower added three years later; King Edward V11 (with pet dog Caesar) was a guest in 1905. The local chimney-sweep dreaded calls to the hotel, as his work has to be done continental-style from the roof downwards. By the 1970s tastes had changed, the once grand building fell derelict and was destroyed by fire in 1976. Mallett Close now stands on the site.

CORSICA HALL Home of the Harben, FitzGerald and Bowes families from the early eighteenth century, in 1886 the hall became Colonel Savage's Seaford College for boys. A game is in progress on the cricket field, site of the former riverbed, now built as the Covers. Since 1940 the college has been at Petworth.

GENERAL VIEWS FROM SEAFORD HEAD Two postcard views from a similar angle show Steyne Road ('Le Havenside') running approximately left to right in the middle distance. Above, Little Steyne (Jubilee Garden), South Street, Seaford House 1 (demolished and rebuilt 1860), Crouchfield and the boys' board school (with Seaside Convalescent Home behind) are recognisable. The lower view features Parliament Row, Marine Terrace and points east, and causeways linking the seafront with Steyne Road and College Road.

EVERSLEY, TELSEMAURE At the seaward end of Dane Road hotels Eversley and Telsemaure offered select accommodation for visitors. Telsemaure was built in 1860 for Major Crook and his family; the Eversley built in 1897 appeared in Seaford's first official guidebook seven years later. The seafront shelter was a commemoration of Queen Victoria's Jubilee: public opinion was divided about the inclusion of its newfangled subterranean public conveniences.

TELSEMAURE, STORM DAMAGE During the First World War, Telsemaure was used as a recreation centre for the many troops in training nearby. The 'Viking' complex now occupies its site. The sea wall suffered through loss of shingle, groynes having been shortened as a wartime economy measure. Damage opposite West View was only one instance of many years' battering by heavy seas.

SEAFRONT, DANE ROAD Steps led to the beach from almost the spot where the Jubilee shelter stood, till severely damaged in a gale in 1940. Sea defence work opposite the Eversley was so disruptive that the company involved, on completion in September 1948, invited the hotel's proprietor to perform an 'opening ceremony' and presented her with a bouquet. The hotel has since been renamed 'Beachcomber'.

SEAFRONT TO EDINBURGH ROAD The first sea wall, built in 1865, lasted only a decade; building of extensive defences began in 1881. These two views across the bay towards Newhaven are a good example of 'the calm before the storm'.

SALTS RECREATION GROUND Not without dissention over the loss of common land where sheep had grazed, in 1923 this low lying 15 acre site was set out as a sports area including Children's Corner with swings, sandpit and 'model yacht and paddleboat pond with a man in constant attendance so that children may play in safety without the constant oversight of their elders'. Today's amusements reflect young people's preoccupation with television and video games.

WEATHERPOINT Pictured here when just completed by local builders Pettitt & Son, this house with other seafront homes, during the Second World War was occupied by gunnery units of the Army, as a defence against the expected invasion. Neighbours were warned to open their windows during practices, to offset shock waves. Renamed 'Beachlands', the house is now a rest home.

WEST PARADE Until a night of storms in September 1935, a row of wooden beach huts had stood on the seaward side of the road. Successors to Mr Simmons' bathing tents, they were tossed around and so badly damaged that, when the road was rebuilt on a rise above the beach, there was enough height to create individual shelters at lower level. Shingle was dumped in front for readiness for the 1989 beach re-charging. The area is now dedicated to Seaford's twinning with Bönningstedt.

SEAFRONT OPPOSITE BRICKFIELD This part of the seawall near Groyne 23 suffered severely at the end of the Second World War; tank traps and other anti-invasion devices had prevented access to the beach and maintenance was impossible. Though a drive by the sea was pleasant on a fine day, Claremont Road (built 1876) and the Buckle by-pass (1964) offered traffic a less hazardous route in rough weather.

BUCKLE INNS Two old cottages knocked together made up the inn, regarded by the people of Bishopstone, Tide Mills and Coastguard Cottages as their 'local', sited close to the water's edge. High seas often flooded down the chimneys, to be swept out again through the open front door. For a few days in 1963 the two inns co-existed before the original was demolished. Near this spot in 1545 Sir Nicholas Pelham (family badge, a buckle) with assorted supporters, repelled an attempted French invasion.

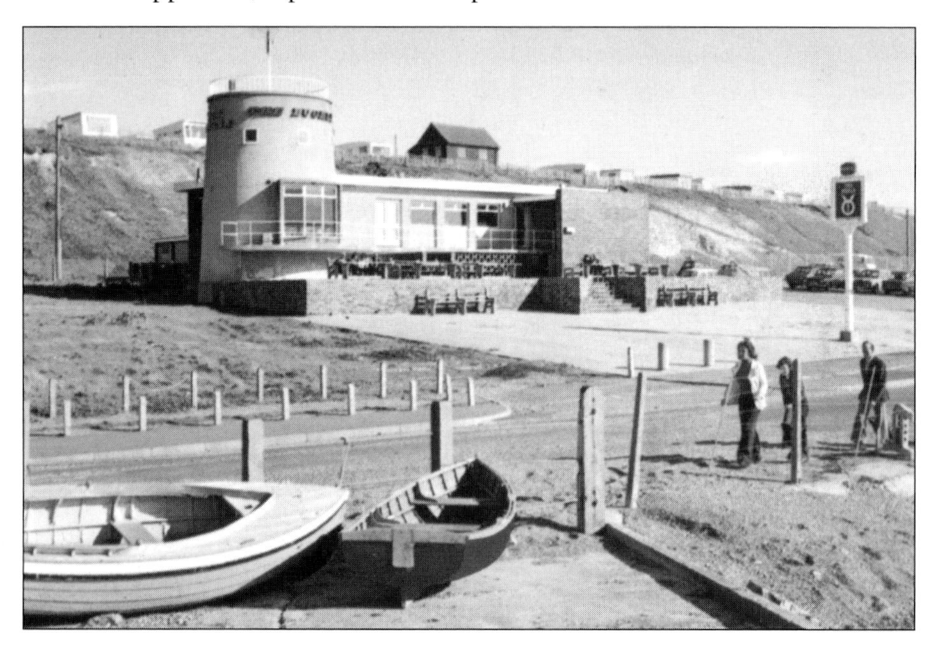

MERCURY MOTOR INN This was a new kind of hotel, designed for motorists, popular in the 1960s-70s. Guests parked at the very door of their chalet and used the bar and restaurant, which had a conference room at the lower level. Fashions changed and by 2004 demolition had taken place, with permitted development of an estate of 24 homes.

CLAREMONT ROAD When the coast road towards Newhaven became too eroded for safety (page 5), Mr Robert Lambe offered land west from Blatchington Road overlooking the railway line (the bridge crossing the track is named after him), now part of the A259 coast road. The station goods yard (far left, lower picture) has now been built over as St. Crispians.

STATION STAFF AND EXTERIOR The first train reached Seaford on 1 June 1864, when the London Brighton & South Coast Railway opened a single-track branch line from Newhaven. By 1905 the station was busy enough to require a large staff including several telegraph operators. The station approach road had gates at each end (Terminus Road - later named Clinton Place - and Claremont Road), symbolically closed once a year, to confirm its private status.

RAILWAY LINE A rare view (upper) of the western gates of Station Approach, fully open to allow a military band to march through en route for the camp site where summer manoeuvres would take place. There are two theories about Seaford's especially long platforms: were they meant to accommodate troops and their equipment and horses...or boarding school pupils and their luggage and tuck boxes?

RAILWAY STATION Though the two photographs were taken nearly a century apart, background features have changed very little. The older L.B.S.C. locomotive has been identified as the A1X 'Terrier' of 1872, rebuilt in 1911, with branch headcode. The latest trains were introduced on the Seaford-Brighton line late in 2002, not without teething troubles.

TERMINUS HOTEL Built to accommodate visitors arriving by train, the hotel's opening coincided with that of the railway station itself. For 140 years it has remained one of the town's principal hostelries, surviving name changes and renovations. In the heyday of the boarding schools, it did a roaring trade on Sundays, when parents took their youngsters out to lunch. After a recent (2004) facelift, it has been renamed The Shore.

3 GLOSTER PLACE The three buildings west of the Terminus were originally called Gloster Place. Number 3, 1930s-60s was occupied by printer and stationer A Skelton, same trade Corbell & Taylor, then Mr Hall's Windmill Café and John Shaw's Lobster Pot Café. At shoulder height in Skelton's window (above) is a display of 'Crest' china, once so fashionable and now so collectable, each piece here bearing Seaford's emblem of Cinque Ports badge or other device. Pelham Place below was one of developer Dr Tyler Smith's first attempts (1866) to turn Seaford into 'a second Brighton'.

SEAFORD BAY LOOKING WEST. 9819

PELHAM PLACE GAP On 5th November 1942 an enemy bomb demolished several houses at the north end of Pelham Place, including local British Legion headquarters. Five people were killed outright and another five injured, including a young girl clerk, trapped for six hours. Visible through the gap created could be seen the Ritz cinema and the Southdown bus garage, later used for sea defence works' machinery.

PELHAM ROAD In due course Welbeck Court and Beach Croft were built to fill the gap resulting from the bombing. On the opposite corner the Ritz cinema, opened in 1936 and playing to capacity audiences during the Second World War, by 1979 was dirty, damp and despondent. It was demolished and a Safeway superstore built on the site in 1986.

LAWN TENNIS An early developer's plan shows a plot of land off Dane Road marked for 'Lawn Tennis'. Remembering her girlhood spent in Seaford, Clementine Hosier (who married Winston Churchill) spoke of playing 'bicycle hockey' with her sister on land opposite their rooms in Pelham Place. At its southernmost point (junction with West Street, now the exit road from Safeway's car park) a war memorial was erected after the First World War, moved to its present site in 1952.

CHURCH STREET / CLINTON PLACE When the railway opened, Clinton Place was known as Terminus Road, for the station was the one place it led to. Apart from changes made when the Station Approach gates were removed - plus the lack of iron balcony railings today (blame the Second World War 'salvage' campaign) - there are few differences between the two scenes, for example the pillar-box on the same site.

CLINTON PLACE CROSSROADS Most buildings can be identified with those in the previous picture; only the lamppost and CCTV pole seem alien. From October 2004 most Claremont Road buildings will be obscured behind 'Claremont Quays', newly built on land left vacant for some forty years. When the proclamations were read in 1901 from Number 3 Clinton Pace (seen here with railway boundary wall in background) the premises had been Seaford Urban District Council offices for four years.

Proclamation of King Edward VII at Seaford

CLINTON PLACE TOWARDS EASTBOURNE Terminus Road renamed - with the opening up of Station Approach and the building of Sutton Park Road, this became Seaford's through road, part of the A259 coastal route. Buildings on the right predated those opposite by some years, being originally a terrace of private houses with only Number 1 intended for commercial use. Horse-drawn carriages awaited the summons from the railway station forecourt, to drive across and pick up 'cab' passengers.

CLINTON PLACE SHOPFRONTS Two examples of high-density window dressing, as was acceptable at the time! Ashby's (Numbers 20-21) later became Collihole's, changing its name but not its trade, while 'the Co-op' (Numbers 15-16-17) it remained to local people, whoever was at its helm. Trees then planted in the gutters would have little chance with today's 'through traffic on the busy coast road.

CLINTON PLACE SOUTH SIDE Many and varied have been the goods sold in the shops eventually occupying the ground floors of this elegant terrace. Mr Oxley's bakery and tearoom with unusual windows at Number 6 (later Curra & Osbourne, tobacconists) was next door to the Southdown bus office with waiting room and left-luggage space. At Number 7 the shop-front of Mr Fusciardi's ice cream parlour (the 'ICP' of fond memory) had curved windows and a sort of serving hatch through which one could buy an ice cream cone while standing on the pavement.

MR PACKER

At Number 9 Clinton Place, Mr Packer carried on his work as a chemist and optician, drawing clients with advertisements as the two shown. Outside his shop trees were planted to grow in the gutter; notice the giant trademark 'specs' and large lamp to cast its light on the window display. For many years post-Second World War the premises continued to serve the same purpose, taken over by Mr JVM (Jim) Tanner.

OPTICAL DEPARTMENT

Oculists' Prescriptions glazed with finest materials.

We adapt accurately fitting frames glazed with the finest crystal lenses.

Speciality in rimless "Fitsu."

OUR FEES are moderate and entire satisfaction is given to our customers.

REPAIRS in any branch of optical work are neatly executed at the earliest possible notice.

Dental Department

Teeth extracted by the modern painless methods.

Fillings and other branches of Dentistry can be arranged by appointment.

GOLD · WORK · A · SPECIALITY

F. E. PACKER, M.P.S.,
9, Clinton Place, SEAFORD.

CONGREGATIONAL CHURCH The Congregational Church moved from premises in East Street to this imposing building on the northwest corner of Clinton Place / Upper Broad Street. The foundation stone (still legible) was laid on 7th December 1877 by Mrs Thomas Crook, known as 'the queen of Seaford' for her help and kindness to the poor of the town. A schoolroom, meeting room and other additions have been made in the years since, and the distinctive spire remains prominent on Seaford's skyline.

'ROSTREVOR' Curved flint walls with bushes above, far right of the previous picture, are repeated far left in this photograph of 'Rostrevor', built by the town's popular Doctor William Pringle Morgan. A plaque to his memory in the parish church describes him as 'for over forty years beloved doctor of this town' without mentioning that he was also a pioneer in the identification and treatment of dyslexia. Other doctors succeeded him living in the house till it was demolished; Caffyns's garage, with apartments over has stood on the site since.

PLACE LANE Wynne's ironmongery has occupied the same premises at Number 3 Place Lane (backing onto the site of the old garden of seventeeth-century Place House) for very many years, with few outward changes taking place. Set slightly back to its left we see Mr Allen's bicycle store and workshop and, beyond that the forge from Mr Woolgar would fire the anvil to celebrate weddings and royal occasions. Across the road, the garage used variously by the Post Office and the local unit of the Territorial Army has now been replaced by three modern shops.

PARISH CHURCH The Parish Church of St Leonard was begun in 1090 in a simple aisleless cruciform and later slightly enlarged, but was almost totally destroyed in cross channel raids. When better times came, the ruins were gradually recycled into a church and tower little altered for three hundred years. Built on a rise and clearly visible from ships in the bay, it served as an aid to navigation and a reminder of religion.

LOOKING NORTH TO PARISH CHURCH Many minor alterations and improvements were made in the first years of the nineteenth century to accommodate a growing congregation, including a chancel 'of truly grotesque appearance'. Within fifty years further enlargement was necessary; as completed in July 1862, there have been few major changes since, though wartime bomb blasts destroyed some stained glass windows. Bombed sites nearby were cleared but not redeveloped at once: in 1969 new police headquarters was built, seven years later a new main post office.

CHURCH STREET AND PARISH CHURCH, SEAFORD. D 12366

NEAR THE CHURCH Demolition of Church Street and Pindar Square properties and clearing the site after the bombing exposed the derelict-looking crypt and folly to public view (see opposite). It was fifty years before modern equivalents of the old cottages were built. The Parish Church had suffered not only bomb damage but also much deterioration from the elements, and repairs and replacements had to be carried out in 2002.

THE CRYPT Until 1994, few people had been inside, but an imaginative scheme promoted by Councillor the late Diana Styles saw the creation of the Crypt Gallery, a brick 'shell' enclosing the original flint building. The vaulted ceiling may have suggested a religious use, but experts say it was the undercroft of a medieval merchant's house. All manner of artistic events take place there now, and life has returned to our oldest surviving secular building.

TOWARDS STEYNE ROAD Slanting left and right across the low-lying former riverbed are embanked St John's Road and the Causeway, connecting the seafront, then as now, with Steyne Road ('Le Havenside'). The local authority eventually banned the redundant railway carriage, which was used as a coffee stall, and the site had other bedraggled spells later.

TOWARDS STEYNE ROAD cont'd. First to be built on the landward corner was the hangar where celebrated local balloonist Henry Tracey Coxwell had his factory; the building was later used as an amusement arcade. In 1945 Champions radio works took over; staff numbers rose from 12 to 250 in six years, warranting a visit by BBC personality Richard Dimbleby for the programme 'Down Your Way'. Later that year, fire destroyed the factory and the site was vacant for over forty years, till Kingswell Court was built.

LITTLE STEYNE Across the picture runs Steyne Road, the old waterfront, the scene of Seaford's great medieval trading days. To the triangle of grass (with lamp post) was brought a drinking fountain paid for by public subscription in commemoration of Queen Victoria's jubilee: its first locations outside the New Inn (Wellington) had created a traffic hazard! Moved again - to the Salts recreation ground for many years - it has now returned to Little Steyne (Jubilee Gardens) where, complete with figures for the hours of the day ranged around it, it was dedicated by Mayor Dr Jill Rosser as Seaford Millennium sundial.

SOUTH STREET Here is a closer look at the buildings seen distantly in the Steyne Road postcard view opposite. Far left, the edge of the house behind the lamppost; those on the right are identified by their rooflines. The central house with trees in the garden was 'Lawn House' owned by Mrs Gorringe who gave part of the garden for the erection of the 'tin chapel', the local Baptist congregation's first place of worship (see also page 68).

SOUTH STREET cont'd. After the move to the new Baptist church in Broad Street in about 1900, single-storey lock-up shops were built over the land in front of the tin chapel. Grocers Ellis & Martin occupied the corner for a number of years, and Brenda's newsagent was one of the last. In 2003 the site was cleared and town houses erected, sympathetically designed in keeping with the ancient heart of Seaford.

LOWER HIGH STREET H.H. Evans's drawing of Lower High Street looking east includes (far left) part of Mrs Gorringe's garden fence, then the elegant pillars of Mr Towner's store. Many of the shop fronts can be identified in the early photograph showing surveyors at work prior to the not altogether welcome installation of drainage in the town centre.

LOWER HIGH STREET cont'd. Chemist Mr F.C. Curran dispensed cures for all ills from his shop at Number 5 High Street; he had another establishment at the Lambe's Bridge end of Claremont Road. Sayers bakery had a Hovis sign above the door, and most of the shops served the same type of goods for many years: some remain so to this day.

LOWER HIGH STREET LOOKING WEST A rare view of High Street looking west from the corner of Broad Street: all buildings on the left are indentifiable today, with only the flint wall of Augusta House (‘Talland ‘ - extreme left) lost when the old house was demolished and Talland Parade shops were built. Next door, the late eighteenth-century house was faced with ‘mathematical tiles’, to give the appearance of a then fashionable brick frontage. The lean-to shop (far right) marks the entrance to Church Lane.

UPPER HIGH STREET The arrival of a photographer from Monsieur Levy's famous studio brought out plenty of High Street residents at the turn of the century! The Old Tree inn, dating from Tudor times, was demolished in 1965 and replaced with modern stores. Other shop fronts have changed little.

UPPER HIGH STREET The tree far right on the previous page appears in the centre of this upper picture; the single storey shop to its right later had an upstairs added. Less than fifty years separate these two views: from a deserted street to one where a little girl and two men can just about walk between the parked cars and vans.

EAST STREET One of the town's oldest streets, this suffered badly when enemy bombs fell during the Second World War; in 1950 modern Council flats were built to replace houses on the west side of the road, destroyed seven years before. The former Congregational chapel, later a laundry, facing down High Street, suffered a similar wartime fate and the site remained vacant for many years (except on Bonfire Night) till eventually redeveloped with today's block of flats.

The Gateway, Crouch Gardens, Seaford.

CROUCH GARDENS Mr Cullingford, a London businessman with a country home at Crouch House, gave part of his garden for public use. It was reached from East Street by way of this stone arch, dating from Tudor times and discovered in 1922 during repairs to the dungeon of the Old Town Hall in South Street and installed here nine years later. For some years Crouch House served as offices for Seaford Urban District Council; it was later demolished and residents of its successor, Coldstream House, now hold fund-raising events in the gardens.

BOWLING GREEN Very little has altered over the years in this immaculate corner of the Crouch Gardens, so near the heart of town; beyond the green lies the football field, home for many years of Seaford F.C.

BROAD STREET When drainage surveyors turned their attention to Broad Street, it was a quiet road with old cottages on its west side and terraces of sturdy town houses opposite. The one commercial exception was the chemist's shop (far right) of Mr L Cameron, seen in the lower picture standing at the kerb assisting a customer confined to a bath chair.

CAMERON'S Cameron's was established in 1855 and has remained a chemist's shop at the same premises ever since, a constant in the changing face of Broad Street. In spite of bombs damaging properties nearby, it has been possible to retain such features as the lamppost with water-trough in its base.

BROAD STREET Trees lining the streets were an attractive feature of Seaford's shopping centre in the early twentieth century, lost it seems during the Second World War and others planted to commemorate Queen Elizabeth 11's coronation. Not one remains now.

GABLE END In 1603 two great houses were built in Broad Street, one on each corner of Place Lane. The more northerly, Place House, fell to the developers in 1935, but the other, Gable End, survived some twenty years longer, with its ground floor rooms converted into shops. Leroy's library and music department carried the latest in gramophone equipment.

BROAD STREET SHOPS On 25 October 1942 two lives were lost when an enemy bomb destroyed part of a terrace of flint faced houses with ground floor shop conversions. These included Mence Smith ironmongers and the Misses Gale and Lower's Embroidery Studio. The premises were rebuilt with brick, the contrast giving a perpetual reminder of a tragic day.

BROAD STREET TOWARDS HIGH STREET Trees in the middle distance mark the location of Shepway, one of Broad Street's last residences. Its demolition and replacement with another parade of shops was a repeat of the pre-war fate of Place House, and completed the commercialisation of the road.

TOWN CRIER Mr Peter White successfully revived the ancient office of town crier in 1977, and continues to attend civic occasions as well as announcing local events, such as the annual switch-on of the town centre Christmas lights. He is seldom called upon, as his predecessors were, to spread the word of a shoal of mackerel in the bay or a shipwreck on the beach.

BAPTIST CHURCH After some years in their tin chapel (page 51) the congregation moved to Broad Street premises where they stayed with added garden and hall, for some 65 years. Music came from a rare Gern organ, passed over the intervening churchyard wall from the parish church donors when they acquired a larger instrument. In 1972 the Belgrave Road church opened and shops were built on the Broad Street site.

SEASIDE CONVALESCENT HOME After only nine years in its original quarters in Lower High Street (page 55) the home needed to expand, moving in 1870 to purpose-built premises off Crooked Lane, where convalescents could be nominated by patrons for a four-week stay, on the road to recovery from illness or surgery.

SEASIDE CONVALESCENT HOME cont'd. The home was thought to be the first of its kind in the country and counted princesses, dukes and bishops among its patrons. It set the example for two other homes, the Surrey and the Bainbridge, inmates of all three hoping to benefit from Seaford's famous sea air. Re-development for housing closed them all in the 1960s: Bramber Close was built on the site of the Seaside Home.

GOLF Golf came to Seaford in 1857 when the first course was laid out, with a nine-hole version for ladies, between Chyngton Road and Seaford Head, where some parts were more than 300 feet above sea level. The original clubhouse was the local shepherd's cottage, but corrugated iron huts soon provided better accommodation. The Dormy House was acquired in 1908 and served as such for nearly sixty years.

GOLF cont'd. When Seaford Head Golf Club opened new headquarters at the course end of Southdown Road, the former premises became a hotel and country club. They were sold in 1988, demolished and houses built, with Bracken Road to the east and the Community College behind.

St. Barnabas, Stafford Road, Seaford.

STAFFORD ROAD 'St Barnabas' later known as 'Stafford House', for some time stood alone on the northeast corner of Broad Street. In 1928 the Union Club moved there from its earlier headquarters in Bay House, Pelham Road; it has been there ever since and celebrated its centenary in 2001. For a time Numbers 27-29 Sutton Park Road stood semi-neighbourless, with views clear across to the Avondale end of Stafford Road.

ST. THOMAS MORE CHURCH Seaford's Roman Catholic community attended the chapel at Annecy Convent till funds were raised to build their own church on the southeast corner of Sutton Road and Highlands Road. The foundation stone was laid in June 1935, only one month after the canonisation of St. Thomas More, to whom it was dedicated.

St Thomas More from Highlands Road Seaford, Sussex.

ST THOMAS MORE cont'd. The church was completed early in 1936, extended 44 years later and its hall added in 1984. The Sisters of Providence, persecuted on the continent early in the twentieth century, found a new home in Seaford, established Annecy Convent and the Sutton Avenue school that exists to this day.

SUTTON CORNER In 1930's guidebooks described as 'Bimbo's Garage and engineering works, Eastbourne Road', post Second World War with the proprietor still Mr T.W. Barfoot, the same premises had become 'Sutton Corner Engineering Works' and the same road 'Sheep Pen Lane'. By then Mr Hackett's Rock Fire Riding Stables had gone, but to the east Mr Moore's Seaford Hunting Stables continued, where local boys could sometimes cadge a ride, delivering a horse to its out-of-town hirer.
('Then' photograph reproduced by kind permission of Mrs D Mullineux)

ALFRISTON ROAD Following a route first trodden in Saxon times (if not earlier), the road from Alfriston to Sutton was in the 1930s part of a major scheme intended to by-pass Seaford town centre, with the 'Seven Sisters' hotel as a roadhouse along the way. The Black Cat stores at Number 39, proprietors at various times being Mr and Mrs Chandler, Mr King, Mr Green and Mr Long, served the neighbouring community until very recent times as grocer's, sub-Post Office - and video shop.

PONDS In ancient times two ponds, possibly the water supply for the nearby leper hospital, were sited on diagonally opposite corners of the Blatchington Hill crossroads. That known as the Lily Pond (though still occasionally making its presence felt) was emptied in the 1930s and built over as Redcourts Sports Club. As Elm Court, it is now firmly established as a youth club centre.

PONDS cont'd. The second pond, with Sutton Drove running parallel to the north, has in living memory varied from muddy puddle to flourishing wildlife refuge, the latter thanks to a group of enthusiasts who raised some £2000 for restoration and since 1980, with expert help and advice, have wrought great change for the better. Small chance now of a repeat of its use as a skating- rink!

East Blatchington, Seaford.

BLATCHINGTON Any one of those who posed for the photographs nearly a century ago would still recognise almost every building in both views: only trees, bushes and greenery have been reduced. Rooflines and chimneys remain much the same; only the snarl of present day traffic has destroyed the tranquillity of a walk through Blatchington village.

F_46862. BLATCHINGTON VILLAGE, NEAR SEAFORD.

BLATCHINGTON cont'd. Behind wrought iron gates fronting Firle Road, Blatchington, the house and former stable block of Alces Place, now elegant homes, add to the dignity and peace of the village. The church, dedicated to St Peter the Apostle, occupies what is considered a pre-Christian sacred site. Its gravestones indicate former celebrated residents including Victorian developer and four times town Bailiff Dr William Tyler Smith and Colonel Coote Manningham, commander of the early nineteenth century Rifle Corps.

SCHOOLS From the late nineteenth century till the outbreak of the Second World War, boarding schools flourished in Seaford's good air and quiet surroundings. The Downs School at Sutton Corner ended more than sixty years' education of girls in 1964, to be taken over as offices for the local Urban District Council, which only a decade later became part of Lewes District. Boys from Kingsmead, established in 1911 off Belgrave Road, went on to become kings, heroes and celebrated athletes, but little of the school was spared when the site was developed at the start of the twentyfirst century.

King's Mead Chapel.

EXCEAT NORTH OF BRIDGE Seen upstream from the bridge in the 1930s, canoes and other small vessels hired from the boathouse (left) made their way towards Alfriston, following the route taken by Stanton Collins and other smugglers and miscreants. The voyage would take them past the white horse landmark cut in the chalk of Hindover Hill, just below the skyline

SFD.67. INTERIOR, THE GOLDEN GALLEON, EXCEAT BRIDGE, SEAFORD

Cuckmere River, Nr Seaford

ON THE CUCKMERE The Golden Galleon began as a school for young ladies interested in a catering career. With its views across the Cuckmere meanders to Friston Forest, the hotel has over the years evolved into a popular venue for those walking the lovely valley and others driving out from Seaford and neighbouring towns.